WALKING INTO THE MORNING

A JOURNEY TO THE OTHER SIDE OF GRIEF

by MARGARET WALPOLE

illustrated by MARY TARA O'KEEFE

The C. R. Gibson Company, Norwalk, Connecticut 06856

I will sing of thy power; yea, I will sing aloud of thy mercy in the morning: for thou hast been my defence and refuge in the day of my trouble.

Psalms 59:16

Death

The suddenness of it all was hard. His death was jarring, shocking, final...so quick it was almost unreal. We were happy one afternoon, and that night he was gone. My strong, healthy, kind, tender, handsome husband was gone.

He was athletic. He played golf and racquetball and usually won. That afternoon he had a racquetball game at five.

"Call me tonight," he'd said as I left to visit our daughter in Greenville. "I'll want to talk to you after the game." I'd called and called and couldn't get through. Our phone was busy. We'd always called when one of us was away and so I'd tried again and then the door opened...

"Daddy's dead," they said. Our wonderful, strong, college sons came to tell us he was dead. No...it can't be...I've just left him. I was just going to talk to him. We were together a few hours ago...

Racquetball...He'd won, then turned to give a thumbs-up signal to friends and fell. The suddenness of it all was agony.

Our oldest son took charge. He called his brother in Florida and arranged for him to fly home. He assigned us to cars, and we left. We got lost, but it didn't matter. My husband wouldn't worry about us anymore. They wanted us at the hospital where they had taken him, so we had to go. But I knew he wasn't there.

We drove; we talked a little; we cried; but my son was in charge. He let me talk; he listened as I reminisced about his dad and how I loved him. What a life we'd had.

Memories...what a parting. Our last words were: "I love you."

"I love you, too."

We had grown to love the other better than self.

Thank You, God, for that. And thank You that our oldest son took charge.

Friends

The doors of the hospital opened, and friends were there. What comfort to see familiar people, to hear their voices, to feel their compassion. They took us to a room and sat with us as forms were signed, permissions given. I asked for his wedding band. Someone brought it to me, and I put it on a chain around my neck and we went home... with his ring.

When we reached our home, more friends were there. They stood as we came in and held us close...friends. They came to weep with us. They loved him, too. They shared their time, their love, their strength. Neighbors, church friends, our deep, close, loving friends were there, and their presence helped so much.

Lord, thank You for friends...the priceless gift of loving friends.

The First Night

There was no sleep...there was no wish for sleep. I wandered around the room that had been ours...touching, looking, remembering.

I read some Psalms:

> *I will lift up mine eyes unto the hills,*
> *From whence cometh my help.*
> *My help cometh from the Lord,*
> *Which made heaven and earth.*

> *Out of the depths have I cried unto Thee...*
> *I wait for the Lord, my soul doth wait.*

I was waiting. Waiting for someone to say it wasn't true. Waiting for him to come back to this home, to this room, to me.

I opened his wallet and read everything inside. I wrote him a letter that I would never mail telling him again how much I loved him, how good he had been for me, how loving, how generous, how kind.

How blessed I am to have been his. I knew that I had been good for him, too. I cherished remembering.

A Man Can Cry

You were away when your father died, son, and it was so hard to tell you and so hard for you to hear. It was hard for you to get on a plane and come home to sadness, funeral home decisions, people all over your driveway, your home, your yard. I know you appreciated the people but it did make reality sink in—and then you saw the newspaper announcements. You saw his picture there and though your heart screamed out to deny it, you knew your dad was gone, and you broke down.

It was all right, son. Crying is manly sometimes. You need not believe that one thinks less of you because of your tears. God doesn't. Your tears were for your greatest loss—your dad, your spiritual leader, your model, your source of earthly strength, security, safety, and love.

Your dad was gone. Where, son? You know where. You now have two fathers, both in heaven.

It's all right for a man to cry. Jesus did.

The Funeral

We wanted it to be a worship service. We wanted to worship the God we believed in, we trusted, we believed. He proved that He had conquered death and He said:

> *Let not your heart be troubled: Ye believe in God, believe also in Me. In My Father's house are many mansions: if it were not so, I would have told you. I go to prepare a place for you ...that where I am, there ye may be also.*

The place for my husband was ready. There was no doubt of that in our minds. His life testified to that, now the way we accepted his sudden death would be our testimony. God would give us strength enough for that.

The organist was playing "How Great Thou Art," when we entered. Our church was full, and friends had gathered at the sides and back and overflowed into the courtyards. Our hearts were full...how much we appreciated their coming, their support in song and prayer, their nearness, their tears. Our minister spoke of God, His control, His promises, and the fact that He doesn't make any mistakes. He spoke of my husband, our children's father and of his faith, his willingness...no, his eagerness to share that faith with everyone he knew...and of his love for God who showed us how to live and how to die, who gave His Son as a sacrifice for us that we might live forever with Him in the dwelling place He prepared for us.

There were tears. There was also joy. The tears and the joy mingled, and we knew the Lord understood.

We hoped the world did.

The First Days

Oh Lord, I'm numb. My legs tremble as I stand, and I am hot and feverish. No one told me, Lord, that death was major surgery and recovery would be slow. These first few days are strange, Lord. You've given me anesthesia, and its after-effects are lingering.

Sounds echo in my head, and I don't take things in. There has been gross amputation, and I want to reach for what's no longer there. Yet You sustain me, Lord. You hold me up. The strength I have is not my own. You carry me. I'm too weak and weary to walk, and You carry me.

Worry

I met with our lawyer about the estate. He came to our house and read the will to us, and then we talked. Business is hard for me. I don't know, can't even guess how I will manage money. But worry seems to belong to some other time—some other place. Material things just aren't important now. People are, but not things. He is beyond the state of having to deal with money. He doesn't worry, why should I?

God takes care of the sparrows and clothes the fields with flowers. I'm sure He will take care of us, too.

Grief

Grief is...coming home to an empty house that was once filled with love and happiness. Being cold and doing without the one who warmed you...reaching for the morning embrace and knowing he isn't there anymore...wanting to communicate little joys, little concerns by telephone, by letters...needing to talk and share and realizing that this sharing is over, his voice is gone...seeing others hug and hold hands and knowing your hugs are gone, your hand is empty...

...eating alone, working alone, shopping for one.

...cooking for one.

...sitting alone in church.

...making decisions by yourself.

...wrenching separation.

...silence.

...brokenness.

...trusting God.

I Don't Know What To Say

I called a friend about some church business, and she was glad to hear my voice—it had been a while—and then she said, "I don't know what to say to you."

How honest...how comforting...that my grief would leave her speechless.

So many people say, "I know just how you feel," and they really don't, but this friend was honest. She felt my loss deeply, as I do. She loves deeply, as I do. And when one loves deeply, one grieves deeply.

She comforted me. I am not ashamed of my grief. I don't know what to say either.

One Day At A Time

Oh Lord, You've shielded me and carried me and given me so much to do that I haven't looked into the future much until today. And now I see some things that are going to be so hard: weekends…holidays…Sunday afternoons.

It isn't pretty, Lord. You've made me look at just a little bit, and I don't like it. I'm glad you aren't making me look at all of it at once. Just a little bit is sinking in, and I'm scared. You have said, *"sufficient unto the day is the trouble thereof."* Is that what "one day at a time" means?

Lord, help me look at just one day. I think I can handle that.

Depression

Incredibly, it's been three months since I've seen him—
the one I love, my husband. Incredibly, I must live the rest
of my life without him. That's hard to believe, hard to bear.
I miss him with every fiber of my being, every hour, every
day, every lonely night. He isn't ever coming back...not
this time. Grief is exhausting, and I am exhausted.

People ask, "How are you doing?" What am I supposed
to say? I am physically fine, spiritually fine, but mentally,
close to self-pity. I put that smile on my face and go on,
but inside I'm eaten up with loneliness, always aching,
always missing him. I'm sick that when I go home he is
never there. I can't call him on the telephone, can't hold
him, can't have him hold me. Brokenhearted is a trite
word compared to this—everything is broken. I ache—
there is no other word.

The Dream

I had such a vivid dream. You were back, and you were holding me. I was warm, and you kissed me. Then I asked, "Why did you leave me...why did you do that to me?" I held on to you as I asked, never to let you go again.

"I don't know," you answered, "but I'll never go again. I promise, I will never, ever, leave you again," and then the dream and you were gone.

I awoke—empty, angry, dejected, bewildered. I wept.

Job's Friends

The minister was powerful from the pulpit. He spoke about the cross, and the sermon was inspiring. My friend wanted me to meet him so we waited after the service, and she introduced me. She told him about my husband's death and he quickly asked, "Well, is God's grace sufficient for you?"

What a question. Doesn't Scripture say that it is? "There is no other Comforter," I answered.

"You know, God is the Husband of the widow and the Father of the fatherless," he said.

How true, but how blunt. Did he want an answer this time? I mumbled something and thought about it all afternoon. Surely this man had known no grief. He was trying to tell me that God should take the place of my husband. I've read that before, but my heart is still broken, my house is so quiet, my arms are empty, and my phone does not ring with his calls, and I am so lonely.

People say that time will heal, but I do not believe that. Does it make sense that I would miss him less the longer he is gone? Be careful Eliphaz, Bildad, Zophar. Don't throw me a sop and expect me to be whole again. Only God does the healing, and I must wait.

Why?

The beach was desolate today. I passed a couple walking together, and my whole being screamed out in loneliness. I asked God why...why He took you and left me here... why He separated us when we loved each other so deeply ...why you...why now...why did you have to die?

I think He answered me. There was no voice...no bright lights...nothing mysterious...just a calming of my soul and the answer in my mind...

"Why not? He belonged to Me. Did you really think that you could go through life without suffering, without loneliness, without pain? Why should you be exempt from suffering?"

No reason, except I loved him so...

"Love Me more."

I do, but differently.

"My grace is sufficient for you. I will supply your every need."

What about desires?

"Sublimate desires."

That's hard, Lord, but evidently it can be done. I trust You will show me how.

The sunset was beautiful as I walked home. The huge, orange sun just dropped below the horizon. There was still a glow...enough to color the whole world at that moment. Like death...even though he is gone, there is still a glow. He colors my whole world.

Deliverance

This afternoon I sat at his desk, looking out into the rain and the grief came in waves, one after another, washing into the hollowness, hitting me relentlessly, making me want to give up and then it lifted, and I looked up.

I'll never forget, Lord. You gave me so much in a husband. I am grateful and blessed. I know he is with You, and You are with me in this sorrow. You've promised deliverance in, not from, tribulation, and Your promises are true. I will always miss him, but You—the God of the universe—You have promised to be with me. I need only to look up to find deliverance.

The Prism

A box came through the mail today, and I opened it. Wrapped carefully inside was a prism...and a string.

"Please hang this in a window that you look out of frequently," said the note. "When the sun comes through in the morning, it will remind you of God's love. Nothing can ever happen to you that hasn't first been filtered through the prism of God's love."

It's just a piece of glass...nothing, without the sun. But when God's light hits it, a myriad of color sparkles forth and dances around my kitchen, coloring my walls and lightening up my world.

We are like that...nothing, without the Son. When His light shines through us, we can brighten up the world. Oh, Lord, shine Your light through me. Let me be a prism for others. Let me reflect a bit of Your light to the world.

Pushing Me On

We jogged together, early in the mornings and loved it. He was much the stronger and encouraged me on. As we neared the end of our route together, (he always ran on for extra mileage) I got tired, and couldn't make it around the bend. Up the last hill was more than I could run, and he put his hand in the middle of my back and pushed me on.

His strength was mine. He gave it freely—he had strength to spare. We were one. We ran as one. His footsteps set the pace for me.

Today I run alone. There are no footsteps to set my pace, no smile of encouragement from him, no joy in being together. Still I tire as the bend approaches, and I can't make the turn.

"Put your hand on my back," I cry, "push me on...I can't make it without you here...can't even make it around the bend!"

And then, by some treat of God's, I feel him there pushing me on. His hand is in the middle of my back, encouraging me, strengthening me. His strength is mine and he is...pushing me on.

Promises

A friend brought me a little book called *Promises*. What a thoughtful thing to do. Everything is right from Your Word but now I have all the promises at my fingertips, and I treasure them. There is so much that I have to do, Lord, but sometimes I need to sit and think of You. You never change, and that is comforting. My whole world has turned upside down and nothing is where it should be but You...You are there. You will never leave me nor forsake me. You promised that, and I cling to Your promises. May Your unfailing love be my comfort according to Your promise to Your servant.

Precious in the sight of the Lord is the death of His saints. My husband's death was precious to You, Lord. Your promises renew my life. You will give me the oil of joy instead of mourning and the mantle of praise instead of the spirit of fainting. Thank You, Lord, for Your promises.

On The Beach

Walking on the beach today is different…not as lonely as last time. I love the beach—the sand cushions my feet, and the wind feels good on my face. The ocean's rhythmic swells and draws are comforting, as a companion would be…back and forth, near and far, loud and soft…the gentle heartbeat of God. I look out over the sand, over the water, and it seems to go on forever. I look up and can see no end to the blue—except where a wispy cloud interrupts.

I find beautiful shells—conch shells, clam shells, white wings. As I start picking them up, I realize that each is more beautiful than the last. There seems to be no end to the shells. As the beach stretches on, the shells form a shadow from the setting sun, but I can see them up ahead, beckoning me on. How many more can I hold? Do I need to clasp them all to myself or can I let go, knowing there will be more tomorrow? I put some down beside a walk-way, hoping someone else will enjoy them in the morning.

While I walk home, my hands dry and become warm again. I watch the sun set in front of me. The huge orange sun, darkened with clouds and filtered, drops behind the world to light up some other place but there is no end to it. I realize again the majesty of God. There is no end to His gifts. Perhaps I need to let go to be able to grasp what He now wants me to have.

I'm beginning to see a glimpse of tomorrow, Lord. I'm not afraid anymore. Your blessings are already there. Help me look for them.

Suffering

Lord, I have a tendency to forget who I am in relationship
to You. You related Yourself to me when You came to this
world as God incarnate. Lord, You suffered so. You could
have shirked the role of suffering love, but You did not.
You realized who You were as God the Father took You
through the years as suffering Servant...and You did not
turn from it. You lived that role for us, even though You
wanted release:

> *Father, if it be possible, let this cup pass from*
> *Me.*

How real, how agonizing, yet You also said:

> *Thy will be done.*

You drank of that cup. You accepted Your suffering, and
now, You want me to accept mine. How I yearn for this
cup to pass from me, but it will not. It cannot. And I must
live with this.
   Surely, Your suffering will give me strength; Your Spirit
will give me comfort; Your triumph will give me joy.
Because of You, there is eternity with God...
Because of You, my husband is more alive than ever...
Because of You, death is conquered forever...
And though Your suffering was immense, I am related to
You in suffering.

My Heart Is Lighter

My heart is lighter. You are healing me, Lord, and I can feel the strength coming...slowly, filling up all the hollow places with another love. What a love this is, Lord. I'm just beginning to understand what You mean by suffering love. My heart goes out to others who are sorrowing in a new way. Every affliction is different, but I can share in their sorrow because of my own.

As You have comforted me in my grief, so I will try to comfort others. As You have loved me through it all, so I will try to love others. But all that is possible only through Your strength, Lord. There is none of my own. Fill me with the strength of Your Spirit so that the hollowness is gone, and You can use me, Lord. I'll never be the same again, but my heart is lighter, Lord.

My Father's Business

The sunshine feels good on my face today. There is a new and noticeable spring in my step and a smile—not a forced one—on my face. There are things to do that I can do well, and I must be about my Father's business.

Even grown children need a mother, and I am the only mother mine have, so I'd best be about that business. There is work to do at church. I am stronger now, and I can be a more giving person there. I have been in one of God's educational programs and the tuition has been high, but there is a mark on me. It says, "She's been there. She survived."

My students need a teacher. They have their own back again, and she's better. She can teach them Beowulf, Chaucer, and Macbeth but she can also teach them that life has its shares of sorrows and joys for every person, and that there are things that have to be worked through. There are no quick fixes that really last.

She will teach them (and anyone else who will listen) that grief is real, and it can be an acceptable companion, but life is there, waiting to be reached for—to be lived with joy and eagerness. Friends are there to laugh with, to love with. Books are there to read, to underline, to quote. Beauty is there in the faces of children, in flowers, in this sunshine. You have told us that joy comes in the morning, Lord. Thank You for this glorious morning.

Scripture

I will hide Thy word in my heart, dear Lord, that I might not sin against Thee. How You have encouraged me through Your Word! When I realize the depths of longing and can stand no more, You speak to me. Through Your Word You speak to me. You call me afflicted and storm-tossed, and You promise my rescue. You tell me about heaven where You will wipe away every tear, and there shall no longer be any mourning; there shall no longer be any death, or crying, or pain. The first things have passed away.

You tell me to sing a new song and to offer new praise. You even put the words in my mouth and the song in my heart. I'm ready, Lord, for whatever You have for me in Your plan. Thank You for speaking to me in Your Word.

Thank You, Lord

There is so much to thank You for, Lord: the wonder of Your love, the wonder of the cross, the wonder of Your presence with me now. You have been by my side for a long time. You have surrounded me with Your angels, and they have protected me. When I could not stand, You carried me.

When I drove up my driveway and could not get out of the car to go into the lonely house, You gave me courage. You made me think of happy times, happy places, happy people. And when I was inside, You caused the phone to ring and placed a cheerful voice on the other end. You have talked to me with verses that at first, I did not want to hear:

> *For our light affliction, which is but for a moment, worketh for us a far more exceeding and eternal weight of glory... far beyond all comparison...*

Compared to eternal glory, his death is momentary. Light? My affliction is light? Yes, light!

> *We look not at the things which are seen, but at the things which are not seen: for the things which are seen are temporal; but the things which are not seen are eternal.*

Thank You, Lord. Thank You.

Walking Into The Morning

You have taught me to walk on my own for a while now—without the numbness, without the fear, without the hollowness—but You are there...ever before me, beckoning me on, ever beside me, walking in fellowship, ever behind me, pushing me on.

The pain has been a prelude to this new strength, new purpose, new closeness to You. What can the future hold that I fear? I have walked the road through the valley, and You have been with me all the way. I have seen the sun set and have recognized the majesty of God. And now I see the morning.

We are on the other side of the valley, and I see the sweeping colors, the pinks and blues, the broad brush strokes of Your making a morning. You have taught me to live again, Lord...but not alone. I see the bright lights, and I am not alone because You are walking with me ...into the morning.

Designed by Mary Tara O'Keefe
Typeset in Garamond Book and
Garamond Book Italic